MW00944097

Forgiveness–
The Key
to Pleasing God

Discover the Secret to a Victorious Life!

By
John F. Scott, Jr.
With Roxanne Ryan

PRESS

Forgiveness The Key To Pleasing God
Discover the Secret to a Victorious Life!
by John F. Scott

Printed in the United States of America

ISBN 9781622308354

Unless otherwise indicated, Bible quotations are taken from The King James Version..

www.xulonpress.com

INTRODUCTION

For a believer, someone who has accepted Jesus as Lord of their life, the most important thing is to please God. When you truly recognize His love for you, expressed through the forgiveness of your sins and the promise of eternal life, you can't help but want to please Him.

This booklet is meant as a guide to help believers realize the importance of the role forgiveness plays in pleasing God – from your first receiving His forgiveness to your pleasing Him by being a forgiver like He is.

To truly understand forgiveness, let's first consider this truth: the God of the universe, the Father of glory, the God of all things is the Forgiver. He forgave the world. He sent His son, Jesus, that we might receive forgiveness through Him. Jesus is the express image of God, the manifestation of forgiveness.

Forgiveness is no ordinary power. It is not the characteristic of the weakling, as some have supposed. Jesus was meek and humble, but meekness and humility of character actually mean strength and courage.

Forgiveness is not only the key that releases the chains of addiction, divorce, abuse, etc., but it is also the key that releases the abundant graces of God: health - freedom from sickness, disease and infirmities; prosperity – freedom from all lack; and soul prosperity – freedom to live in love, joy and peace. Jesus is our forgiveness and our example for how to forgive. If you've been looking for a formula for forgiveness, you're reading the right book.

In my years of experience as a minister of the Gospel and a chaplain, I have seen the powerful impact the understanding and application of forgiveness can make in the lives of those who want to be all that God has called them to be.

As for me, I personally believe that Jesus Christ is the Son of God, and that God has raised Him from the dead. I confess Him as Lord of my life. My fervent desire is to please Him. He is my entire being, and He is the substance of all that I have, all that I am, and all that I ever hope to be. Jesus is my Lord.

Jesus said that if I ask anything of the Father in His Name, He will do it. Therefore, I expect results from your reading of this book.

If the biblical principles revealed and discussed in this book are true (and I believe that they are), then the same anointing can come upon you as you read it as came upon me as I wrote it, and God will confirm His Word with signs following.

This is my prayer for you:

Father,

To truly please You, we must understand forgiveness, because You are the Forgiver. I pray for all who read this message, that the eyes of their understanding will be enlightened, that their ears will be opened.

Lord, may they be willing and obedient to please You, by reflecting Your image and being forgivers, doing Your will, for Your glory, through the Name and the precious blood of our Lord Jesus Christ.

Amen.

FORGIVENESS
THE KEY TO PLEASING GOD
Discover the Secret to a Victorious Life!

CONTENTS

SECTION ONE

FORGIVENESS IS THE KEY

Chapter One

GOD IS THE FORGIVER

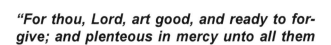

"For thou, Lord, art good, and ready to forgive; and plenteous in mercy unto all them that call upon thee' (Psalm 86:5).

Forgiveness is the key to pleasing God. To truly understand forgiveness, let's first consider this truth: the God of the universe, the Father of glory, the Creator of all things is the Forgiver. As the scripture above plainly states, He is always, perpetually and forever, ready to forgive. The mercy and grace of God is shown most clearly through His primary act of forgiveness, when He forgave everyone in the world. He sent His son, Jesus, that we might receive forgiveness through Him.

Why was it necessary for us to be forgiven in the first place? The Word tells us in 1 John 2:12, that our sins are forgiven for His sake. Adam's original sin robbed us of the perfect spiritual inheritance God was determined for us to have, and left us with the natural inheritance of a fallen nature. So forgiveness was necessary, for God's own sake, so that His desire for us to be like Him could be fulfilled.

No matter how hard God's created beings tried to atone for their own sins, they just couldn't make it work. So, out of His vast love, He put into effect the eternal plan that would provide forgiveness for us:

"For God so loved the world that He gave His only begotten Son, that whosoever shall believe in Him will not perish, but have everlasting life." (John 3:16)

Then, knowing that even after our salvation we would sometimes forget the sacrifice made for us and stumble into sin, He made provision for that:

"If we confess our sins, he is faithful and just to forgive us our sins, and to cleanse us from all unrighteousness," (1 John 1:9).

He Is Who He Is

The bottom line is this: God is love, and His love is so complete, so unconditional, so marvelous that, as the highest possible expression of love against a suffered wrong, He forgave and continues to forgive.

God is the Forgiver. You can't separate someone from who he is. Forgiveness is as much a part of our Heavenly Father's character as are His mercy, His grace, His lovingkindness, His virtue – everything that He is.

That's why it is so important for those of us who have the privilege of a personal relationship with the Creator of the Universe, those who are born again of His Holy Spirit, to embrace forgiveness. It is an integral part of our awesome Heavenly Father – the Forgiver – and it pleases Him when we walk in His image.

The Word tells us that we were created for His pleasure. That means that, above all else, we should fervently desire, even crave, the opportunity to please Him. Pleasing Him should be our foremost goal, once we truly grasp the awesome gift of His sacrifice, His forgiveness to us through Jesus, who bought our eternal life.

It is because we love Jesus, and are so grateful for His incredible sacrifice for our salvation, that we must learn to recognize, understand, and learn to operate in the forgiveness that He is. Then we can act just like Him.

Chapter Two

MADE IN HIS IMAGE

"And God said, Let us make man in our image, after our likeness" (Genesis 1:26).

To best understand God's love, and the importance of His forgiveness, we first need to understand our importance to Him. Yes, that's right. As hard as it sometimes is for our minds to grasp, we are actually important to the Lord!

One of the most powerful scriptures in all of the Bible, I believe, is Genesis 1:26, as quoted above. These few words define our relationship with God. In this one verse, we can discover who we are, who God is, and what we can do.

We, you and I, are made in His image!

God is the creator. We are the created. He declared in Genesis 1 that everything that produces anything produces after its own kind:

> *"...the herb yielding seed, and the fruit tree yielding fruit after his kind,...great whales and every living creature after their kind" (Genesis 1:11,21).*

Reflecting His Image

When He said "Let us make man in Our image…" He was essentially saying "after His kind."

I like to talk in pictures to clarify things. Let's look at it this way. If I was an artist and took out my sketching pencil to draw a self-portrait from my driver's license photo, when I completed the sketch, who would it look like? Me, right?

Well, when God began to make man, He looked at Himself and made man in His image and after His likeness. So, when He finished, who did man look like? God, right? And it pleased Him. He wanted to create a people to show forth His praise, His pleasure.

Of course, because of Adam's original sin, mankind stopped acting like God. That's one reason He chose, in His great love for us, to use the forgiveness that stems from that love to send Jesus - so we would have another chance to reflect His loving, forgiving image.

> *"For God so loved the world, that He gave His only begotten Son, that whosoever believeth in Him should not perish, but have everlasting life"* (John 3:16).

Our Body is Just a Shell

People, even in the Church, sometimes get confused because they think that being made in His image and after His likeness has to do with race, nationality, skin color, hair texture, gender, etc. But God's not concerned with all that. He simply created us with the outer shell that was best suited to adapt to the life He destined each of us to live while we're here on earth.

Scripture says that God is a Spirit, and that man is also a spirit. I like the way I've heard some people express it, "Man is a spirit, he has a soul, and he lives in a body."

That says it pretty well.

So it's not our physical bodies that are created after God's image, because He is not a physical body, He is Spirit. Our bodies are just the "shell" or housing that God created for our soul and our spirit (which is in His image) to live in while we're here on earth.

But we have this treasure in earthen vessels, that the excellency of the power may be of God, and not of us" (2 Corinthians 4:7).

Chosen Before the World Began

As amazing as it is to realize you were made in His image, isn't it just as amazing to think that God had planned your life even before the events in Genesis 1?

The Word tells us that before the foundation of the world, you were chosen (see Ephesians 1:4). You and I were predestinated to the praise of the glory of His grace.

Just think about that for a minute. Before Genesis 1:1, you were chosen. Before Adam, the first man, the father of all mankind, you were chosen. Before the stars, the sun, the moon, the planets and the galaxies were put into place, you were chosen…and predestinated into the adoption of children by Jesus Christ unto Himself according to the good pleasure of His will (see Ephesians 1:5,11).

You are adopted for His pleasure! You are special and then some—in fact you are much, much more.

Loving Preparations for the Blessed Event

Again, let me "paint a picture." Look at a woman who's just found out that she's pregnant…a baby is on the way. Almost immediately she begins to set up a special room, a special place, filling it with bright and wonderful things for the baby that's to be born.

The room may be furnished with some bright pastel colors, maybe some special wallpaper. A bed, clothes, diapers, bottles, and various stuffed animals are bought, along with other items to make baby feel safe and happy. The mother does this because she is excited about the expected child, because she loves him or her already, before they are even born.

Some of the items lovingly prepared and put in place are necessary, some are not.

Some are just for the baby's enjoyment and the mama's enjoyment of the baby.

Now look at what God did in Jesus before Adam was created physically. He created an earth and placed a sun, moon, and stars in the heavens to give light. He filled the earth with all the vegetation and animals, all for man's pleasure and sustenance.

God lovingly prepared a world for you to be born into. After all, you are created in His image. You are special. You are not an accident.

Your life might have been a surprise to some people, perhaps even to your parents, but you were not a surprise to the God who lovingly created you in His image and knew you even before you were in your mother's womb (see Jeremiah 1:5).

> **GOD LOVINGLY PREPARED A WORLD FOR YOU TO BE BORN IN...YOU ARE NOT AN ACCIDENT**

Rejoice! You are fearfully and wonderfully made, in God's own image! (see Psalm 139:14).

It is precisely because of this careful, loving way you were created that God's desire is for you to maintain His image. He is a holy God, and wants nothing less for you:

"Because it is written, Be ye holy; for I am holy" *(1 Peter 1:16).*

Being a forgiver is a giant step toward acting in His holy image and pleasing Him by being like Him.

Chapter 3

NO ORDINARY POWER

Before we can go into all that forgiveness is, and its importance in pleasing God, we must first consider the inherent power of forgiveness. We must recognize that forgiveness is no ordinary power.

It is the very power of our Almighty God, the Forgiver.

How does God choose to show me His love for me? How does He prove His love for you? He shows both His love and His power through His forgiveness. It is the tool God has chosen to prove His love.

> **FORGIVENESS...**
> **THE HIGHEST ACT**
> **OF LOVE AGAINST**
> **A SUFFERED**
> **WRONG**

Forgiveness is no ordinary power. It is the highest act of love against a suffered wrong. It is our all-powerful expression of who He is and how much He loves us.

When we have received the forgiveness bought by the blood of Jesus by accepting Him as our Lord and Savior, all the power of God's forgiveness is available to us through the Holy Spirit, who comes to live within us.

It is right there, within us. We just need to choose to exercise it. The first step will be recognizing God's love.

"Jesus Loves Me"

As a small boy, I remember hearing the song, *Jesus Loves Me*. At that time, hearing the song meant there was someone out there beyond my parents who loved me. Now the song has taken on a far greater meaning. I had a child-like basic faith in the fact that the words were true when I was a child, but I didn't grasp what the truth and power of God's forgiving love meant, because of my limited experience and understanding.

Now I am a grown man who has recognized his own inability to run his own life, and who has experienced the saving grace and amazing love of God. I have seen the love of Jesus work wonders in my own life and the lives of others. Today the simple words, "Jesus loves me," bring a powerful reminder of the revelation I have been given of the depth of His love.

> **I MUST KNOW DEEP DOWN THAT HE LOVES ME, OR I WILL MISS ALL THE BLESSINGS HE HAS STORED UP FOR ME**

You see, I needed to know deep down inside that Jesus loves me, that He expresses that love through forgiveness, and what that means to my life.

Until I realized this great truth, I couldn't really receive all the blessings and benefits He had for me within His marvelous forgiving love.

Getting a Good Fit

It's like having a room full of brand new shoes and boots for both men and women, valued at $800 to $1000 a pair. But if all those men's shoes were sizes nine, ten and eleven, they would do me absolutely no good because I wear a size twelve and thirteen. I couldn't get a good fit.

It's the same with Jesus. It doesn't matter how loving

I think He is to someone else, or how well He 'fits' them, if I don't realize that He loves me and will also fit my life into His. I must know deep down that He loves me, or I will miss all the blessings He has stored up for me.

God's power to forgive is no ordinary power. The true beauty of that is that He loves me so much that He's equipped me with the same extraordinary power. Nothing gives Him greater pleasure than for me to use this power and become a forgiver, like He is.

God's done so much for me and loves me so much. There is nothing I can do to repay Him for all He has done, except to make every effort possible to please Him.

Forgiving is who He is, and being like Him pleases Him, so my desire is to become a forgiver. He's given me that power; now all I have to do is be obedient to use it.

PLEASING GOD BY COMING FULL CIRCLE

1.
FORGIVENESS –
God's highest
expression of love
against a
suffered wrong

2.
FORGIVENESS
causes LOVE
to work

3.
LOVE causes
FAITH to work

4.
LOVE works
through
FORGIVENESS

5.
By FAITH we
please God by
being forgivers

WE HAVE COME
FULL CIRCLE
& GOD IS
PLEASED

Chapter 4

THE GOLDEN CHAIN

I once heard a preacher say, "The Word of God is so simple you that have to have help to misunderstand it." I believe that is so true, but I also suggest that we've had a lot of help from our unrenewed flesh and from the enemy to get us to <u>MIS</u>understand.

The fact of the matter is that we often don't take advantage of all the wonderful truth and blessings given to us in the Word and apply them to our everyday walk. We can't fully understand the authority we can have over our own situations, unless we let the Word teach us how to operate in the Spirit of God.

Let's look at it like this. I have two dollars in my front pocket. Someone blesses me with a $20 bill and I put it in my back pocket, but then I forget it is there. I am hungry and go to a supermarket with two dollars in my front pocket. How much food could I buy?

How much money do I have altogether? Twenty-two dollars, right? But how much food can I buy? I can only buy two dollars worth, even though I really have twenty-two dollars, because I've forgotten about the other twenty dollars. But I'm hungry. Does that make a difference? No.

You see, I was blessed with enough money to buy a T-bone steak from a fine restaurant, but as long as I have forgotten about the twenty dollars available to me in my back pocket, I'll have to settle for half of a sandwich and a cup of water, and I'll still be hungry. But I couldn't blame my hunger on the one who blessed me with $20.

How much of the Bible did God give us from Genesis to Revelation? All of it, or just a portion? You'd have to agree that He's given all of it, wouldn't you? Well, how much are you using—two dollars worth or the whole thing?

Our "back pocket" is loaded, but unless we keep reminded of it, and use it, then it's not going to be any help for us. And it's not God's fault. Why am I mentioning all this? Because the answer to finding forgiveness, and being an instrument of forgiveness, is right in front of us – in the Word.

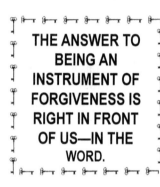

THE ANSWER TO BEING AN INSTRUMENT OF FORGIVENESS IS RIGHT IN FRONT OF US—IN THE WORD.

Let's take it out of our back pocket and put it to use!

Discovering the "Golden Chain"

Let's think of our Christian walk, our walk of faith and love, as links in a gold chain, with forgiveness as the key that holds the chain together.

I'll go into the individual links of the chain in more detail in later chapters, but for now I want you to get the big picture of this "golden chain." It is a chain God has formed in His Word and given to us to show us how to first receive, then use, the key of forgiveness.

Let's start at the beginning:

"For God so loved the world that He gave His only begotten Son that whosoever believeth on Him should not perish but have everlasting life" (John 3:16).

This "chain" begins with God's FORGIVENESS toward us, by the sacrifice of Jesus on the cross for our sins.

When we first begin to appreciate the truth and beauty of God's love in providing for our salvation, we find we want to please Him. So then I looked further into the Bible to learn how to please Him.

"But without faith it is impossible to please Him: for he that cometh to God must believe that He is, and that He is a rewarder of them that diligently seek Him" (Hebrews 11:6).

"Now faith is the substance of things hoped for, the evidence of things not seen" (Hebrews 11:1).

This faith allows us to come to Him so we can access and rejoice in the hope of eternal life.

"Therefore being justified by faith, we have peace with God through our Lord Jesus Christ: By whom also we have access by faith into this grace wherein we stand, and rejoice in hope of the glory of God" (Romans 5:1-2).

I see, then, that His Word says that without faith it's impossible for me to please God. I've learned that my forgiving pleases Him, so, if I really want to please God I must operate in faith and become a forgiver.

Faith in the power of that forgiveness allows us to believe that Jesus died for our sins.

Faith Works By Love

Then, if I look further into the Bible, I see that this faith that it takes to please God works by something. The scripture tells us that nothing else really counts for much,

"...but faith which worketh by love" (Galatians 5:6b).

My purpose is to please God, but I can only please Him by faith, which has to work by love. And what is the most powerful demonstration of love? That's right, forgiveness.

Now can you see the "chain" forming? I want to please God. I can only please Him by faith, which works by love, which works by forgiveness. We'll talk more about each link of this chain, but we need to grasp the totality of it.

It is a beautiful unbroken chain, with FORGIVENESS AS THE KEY that links it all together.

Chapter Five

THE TEAMWORK OF FAITH & HOPE

The "Golden Chain" starts with the love of God shown through the act of forgiveness. Everything starts with His forgiveness. It is that love that gives us hope. Hope for a future, hope for an eternity with Him.

Hope, the creative or imaginative part of this "Golden Chain," is the forerunner to faith.

The Bible tells us:

"Faith is the substance of things hoped for, the evidence of things not seen" (Hebrews 11:1).

Faith is the substance. Faith is evidence. So, faith is the substance of things. What things? Things hoped for, things not yet seen. So the "things hoped for" are the goals. Our goal is to please God. We know that becoming a forgiver like He is pleases Him. We know that without faith it is impossible to please Him. So we know faith is vital if we are to please God and become a forgiver.

Faith and Hope Work as a Team

We see in the above scripture that faith and hope work as a team.

We all have faith. The Word tells us that God has given "every man the measure of faith" (Romans 12:3). It doesn't specify "every believer," but everyone. We all have faith, which means that we all have hope. Hope is strong, orderly, arranged, and purposeful.

Faith and hope work as a team—you can't have one without the other. Faith can't work without hope, and hope is useless without faith. There's no work faith can produce without hope because hope is the object of faith, or the focus or attention of faith.

Faith is Real

Remember, faith is just as real as the chair you are sitting in, the bed you are lying on, or the floor you are standing on. Faith is real.

Touch your chair, the bed, or the floor. Are they real to you? Of course they are. They are substance.

FAITH IS FOREVER SEEKING TO BRING TO PASS... HOPE MUST BE BROUGHT TO PASS..

Faith is more real than that chair, that bed, or that floor.

You might ask, "How can that be?" There answer is: simply because everything that we see was first seen and appeared very real in the eyes of faith.

Faith Makes Hope a Reality

Faith and hope work together as a team to build you up in your spirit man, so that you can begin to operate as God has always intended you to, as a forgiver, made in His image.

"Through faith we understand that the worlds were framed by the word of God, so that things which are seen were not made of things which do appear" (Hebrews 11:3).

Even your belief in God as the Creator is evidence of your faith.

As we focus on the Word of God, the Spirit of God

(the Comforter) creates hope. Faith causes that hope to come to pass. One of God's lawws is that faith must make hope come into reality. Faith will always produce – it's the law

According to the biblical account in 1 Corinthians 13:13, faith, hope, and love abide – that is to say they always exist. Can that be proven from the Bible? Yes, I believe it can. The Bible calls itself the Word of faith (see Romans 10:8). It also states that the Word is God and that God is love (see John 1:1; 1 John 4:16).

Finally, it says that Jesus is our hope, Jesus is the Word and the Word is God.

Eternal Attributes of God

Since faith, hope and love are attributes and graces that reflect the very personality of God, and God is eternal, then faith, hope, and love are also eternal and abide forever. Faith, hope, and love are in each word of the Bible at the same time. Therefore, the Word itself is the word of faith, hope, and love. Praise God!

Since faith is always working, it is our responsibility to give faith something positive to work toward, something good to hope for. Once you realize that faith is going to bring something to pass, you want to direct it toward something you desire – natural or spiritual. We want to direct it toward a walk of forgiveness.

Hope – Seed Planted in the Soil of Faith

Some people misuse the faith they have been given. They have faith to expect bad things to happen to themselves, and faith always produces. If you don't give it something good, it will bring to pass something you don't desire.

Another description might be to liken faith to a check, and hope to the money in a checking account. The money is real, the money has purpose, and the money belongs to you. But to spend that money, you need to have the check.

When you want to purchase something with your money, the check has no value of its own, but is necessary to access the funds. Likewise, if there is no money in the account, the check is useless.

Making the purchase and reaping the harvest requires both the seed (or currency) of hope and the soil (or check) of faith.

REAPING THE HARVEST REQUIRES BOTH THE SEED OF HOPE AND THE SOIL OF FAITH

Believing is Seeing

There is a saying, "Seeing is believing," but faith says, "Believing is seeing."

If, for example, I bought a car and came looking for you to announce to you, "I just bought a new car," you might question me. You might hope I was serious, but be a little skeptical and ask, "Did you really?" Then I could show you my bill of sale and you could rejoice with me.

Faith is like that bill of sale. It is the evidence that convinces you that the thing you hope for is real, even though you haven't seen it yet.

Faith is the builder. Hope is the architect. The builder would have nothing to build without the architect.

Hope sees the end product from the beginning (not the process) as already done. Faith takes the vision of the completed product (you as a forgiver) and walks it through the process. There's always the process. It's part of that "law of production" we mentioned earlier.

"...first the blade, then the ear, after that the full corn

in the ear" (Mark 4:28).

Hope is defined as a desire and earnest expectation. Nothing happens without hope - the desire to be, to do, and to have.

It is the picture, the idea, the ideal, the creative part, the act of creating in the imagination of the mind what is to exist or present itself to the natural world.

Hope thinks, imagines, visualizes, dreams, expects to have, anticipates, and desires, then writes the vision.

You Can Forgive

The choice, the command, to forgive is a true indication that you can forgive.

This book is a step of faith that people I've never met will find the hope that they need to be forgivers, like their Heavenly Father.

Once acted upon by faith through prayer, hope never changes its mind. If hope is changed it becomes double-minded and then, according to James' warning in James 1:7, we cannot expect our prayers to be answered.

It is said that you can live a short time without food, a lesser time without water, a few minutes without air, but no time without hope.

You must hold hope steady, like Abraham did, so as to not give in or give up on what you are hoping for. The choice, the command, is always there. If there is no choice, there is no opportunity to walk in faith. Abraham, when "against hope believed in hope that he might become the father of nations" (Romans 4:17), made such a choice.

God gave Himself to Abraham in Word form. Faith, hope and love are in the same word. Abraham had no doubts. He didn't consider his body or the deadness of Sarah's womb.

Becoming What You Think

His faith in God's Word brought the promise to pass. It is impossible not to hope. If you think, you hope.

Then you become, or accomplish, what you think (hope). It's automatic.

Consider the Scripture that warns that if a man looks upon (thinks about) a woman with lust, he has already committed adultery with her in his heart (see Matthew 5:28).

IF YOU THINK IT, YOU'LL BELIEVE IT. IF YOU BELIEVE IT, YOU'LL SAY IT. IF YOU SAY IT, YOU'LL GET IT.

This is not just a statement of condemnation, but also an example of the power of the ability to think, hope, imagine, and dream that God has built into every person He created.

There are thousands of thoughts going through our minds daily. But you can't use those thoughts you are thinking until you begin to hope.

The Expectation of Hope

Hope is the orderly arrangement of thoughts consciously thought out and expected to materialize.

If you think it, you'll believe it. If you believe it, you'll say it. If you say it, you'll get it.

Thinking (hope) creates it, believing it (faith) gives it substance, and saying it, or praying it, calls it into being.

For example, what do I desire (hope for)? I desire a red car with a red steering wheel, red seat covers, red tires, red wheels and a red hood ornament. Can you see my red car? I know you can.

I can't get my red car, however, until I add my faith to

it. Because hope alone has no substance. But I would never know I desired a red car unless I first thought about it and let my imagination progress into visions and dreams (hope) of my red car. Now I have created a desire, a determination (faith) to possess, own, and have it.

Then comes the "works." Faith without works is dead (James 2:17), so now comes my responsibility to save up for it, shop for it, and purchase it. I <u>became</u> the owner of my red car.

Relating All This to Forgiveness

Do you see how this same progression, the teamwork of faith and hope, relate to forgiveness?

I desire (hope for) a lifestyle of forgiveness to please God. But my hope has no substance until I add faith. Then I develop a determination to see it come to pass. I study the examples in the Word, I determine to surrender and walk in His Holy Spirit, and I finally attain it!

It is because of God's faith in us, and hope for our spending an eternity with Him, that out of love He <u>is</u> a FORGIVER. We will see how that same progression will be our pattern for pleasing God by <u>being</u> FORGIVERS.

Reviewing Key Points – Section I

1. As a believer, _____ God should be our foremost goal.

2. Psalm 86:5 tells us that God is always, perpetually and forever, ready to _____

3. God is a Spirit, and we are made in His image: "Man is a _____, he has a_____ , and he lives in a _____."

4. What Scripture tells us that we were chosen before the foundation of the world?_____

5. Forgiveness is the highest act of_____.

6. _____is the very power of our Almighty God.

7. I can only please God by_____.

8. Faith works by_____ which is expressed through_____.

9. Reaping the harvest requires both the seed of_____ and the soil of_____.

10. It is because of God's_____in us, and_____ for our spending an eternity with Him, that out of_____He <u>is</u> a FORGIVER.

SECTION II

BECOMING A FORGIVER

Chapter Six

HOW CAN I PLEASE GOD?

It's one thing to acknowledge that we want to please God, and that God, the Forgiver, is pleased by our becoming forgivers in His image. It's another to live our day-to-day lives in a way that pleases Him.

We've talked a lot about what God expects and even commands. It is important to know these things if we want to please Him. We've agreed that pleasing God will require operating in forgiveness. All we've talked about and referenced in the Word so far is great, but until we discover how to put it into practice in our everyday life, it's only theory.

"I beseech you therefore, brethren, by the mercies of God, that ye present your bodies a living sacrifice, holy, acceptable unto God, which is your reasonable service.

"And be not conformed to this world: but be ye transformed by the renewing of your mind, that ye may prove what is that good, and acceptable, and perfect, will of God" (Romans 12:1,2).

How can we, living in these unpresented bodies run by an unrenewed mind in this sinful world, actually be forgivers and please Him? That's where the rubber meets the road.

First, we have to acknowledge that as hard as it may

sound, it is possible. God never asks us to do anything, or expects anything from us, that He is not ready, willing, and able to accomplish. Notice I didn't say that WE are able to accomplish. There are many things, including being forgivers, that we are just not capable of in ourselves. But He gives us an awesome promise in His Word that we may not have yet fully comprehended:

"Faithful is he that calleth you, who also will do it" (1Thessalonians 5:24).

This is an exciting piece of Scripture! It is reminding us that God, who is the One calling us to be forgivers, will be the one who will cause it to happen – not us!

All it will take, ultimately, is a surrendering of our will to His, allowing Him to do the work necessary in us so we will be true forgivers like He is.

THE GOD WHO CALLS US TO BE FORGIVERS IS THE ONE WHO WILL CAUSE IT TO HAPPEN—NOT US

Oh, how it pleases Him when we let Him do what He needs to so that we can fulfill our destiny in Him!

The Free Will to Say 'No'

God did, however, give us a free will. That means that we can allow Him to change us, allow Him to help us become all He wants us to be, or we can say, "No."

We can allow Him to bring healing and deliverance in some areas of our life, and keep some areas "off limits," so to speak, to His intervention. Unfortunately, this is what sometimes happens when it comes to unforgiveness.

We love the Lord, want to please Him, have allowed Him to change many of our attitudes, sinful habits, and destructive lifestyles, but have held on to certain hurts, wounds and betrayals.

At some level, sometimes consciously, sometimes unconsciously, we have tried to "cover over" or "bury" the bitterness, grief, sense of unworthiness, and anger that accompanied these hurtful situations.

When this happens, we end up being pulled, as if we were in a tug of war, between our flesh and our spirit. In our heart we want to please God, because we love Him and are grateful for all He's done.

But our unrenewed mind likes feeding on all those negative emotions, and we just don't want to give up our "righteous indignation" (which isn't righteous at all by God's definition) or our perpetual pity party over past or present offenses.

The Instability of Double-Mindedness

The Word warns us that we cannot afford to be "double-minded" (see James 1:8). It likens a double-minded person to someone who can be tossed back and forth, never settling on the truth. It calls a double-minded person "unstable" in all ways. That means that when we allow ourselves to be "double-minded" on the subject of forgiving an offense, we are unstable in all other aspects of our walk with God, too.

The hardest part of that piece of scripture is where it says that a double-minded person can't expect anything from God.

When we're operating in the Spirit, not fulfilling the lusts of the flesh (which is what that resentment we're harboring really is), we can expect God to hear and answer our prayers. But when we are being double-minded, we can't count on the same results. That doesn't mean that God doesn't love us, or can't bless us if He chooses to; it's just that we can't use our faith to expect it.

This book was written to help those in this situation realize that if you truly want to please God, if you truly want a close walk with Him, if you truly want to be used to the fullest for His glory, then choosing to forgive is the only real answer.

Addictions Don't Please God

God loves us, right? Can we, by any stretch of our imagination, think that our addictions and other fleshly bondages are okay with Him, that we can please Him and be prisoners of drugs, alcohol, gambling, or pornography, for example?

MOST BONDAGES ARE NOT REALLY THE ROOT ISSUE, BUT BY-PRODUCTS OF UNFORGIVENESS.

Addictions, like any other sinful lifestyle, can't separate us from the love of God, but they can separate us from a relationship with Him that is intimate and pleasing to Him.

Many of the terrible bondages people are in today, even some Christian men and women, are not really the root issue. Most are actually offshoots, or by-products, of unforgiveness.

The Enemy Takes Advantage

Most didn't wake up one morning and say, "I'm going to have this drink and keep on drinking until I become an alcoholic," or "I just can't wait to stick needles in my arm, or shove some powder up my nose, so I think I'll become a drug addict." Nor did they say, "I think I'll see what I can do today to displease God."

The enemy took advantage of that bitter root of their unforgiveness and used it to convince them that the best they could do is "numb" themselves, or reject everything good and clean and do whatever the world presented as an alternative.

Forgiveness - the Key to Deliverance

Many have bought the lie and settled for a lifestyle of bondage, virtually thumbing their nose at the very God who loves them and wants them to receive forgiveness and a new life.

God's power to forgive is just as readily available to someone who has been bound in unforgiveness, followed by addictive or destructive behavior, as it is to the one whose bondage has been pride, self-gratification, greed, or lust.

Deliverance ministry is great and has its place, but as simplistic as it sounds, many bondages can be broken as easily as truly receiving the forgiveness God so freely offers in Jesus, choosing to please God by being like Him, and forgiving those whose sin has held them in bondage.

God the Loving Father

God didn't refer to Himself as "Father" for no reason. He wants a personal relationship with us. The very first thing any of us can do to please God is believe He really is the loving, forgiving Heavenly Father that He is.

Think of our relationship with our own children. We love them and want wonderful things for them. As they grow and begin to walk out their destiny, we want to be right there with them, doing all we can to encourage, build up, and help them. But when they begin to live a sinful, destructive, or dangerous lifestyle, we can't walk alongside them as if everything is fine.

We love them too much to help them hurt themselves, so we have to love them from a distance, knowing to help them could cause them further damage.

We continue to live our godly lifestyle in front of them as much as possible, giving them a stable standard to look to, and continue to love them, hoping for the day they will come to the point where we can walk alongside them again.

Protected From His Blessings

This is how God looks at us. He will do all He can to help us and protect us, as long as we're walking in the right direction. When we stray, He can't be as involved in our life, because to bless us when we are determined to use the blessing for destructive purposes, would be counterproductive.

You might say He protects us from His blessings so they can't be misused to destroy us. Like when He cast Adam and Eve out of the Garden.

He still loves us, keeps reminders of His standards and His blessings in front of us, and waits with open arms for us to return to Him so He can give us the abundant blessings He has always had ready for us. He is the Forgiver, standing ready to forgive, and is, oh, so pleased when we let Him.

How can you please God? You have to be willing to receive His forgiveness and face any unforgiveness in your heart and let Him deal with it. Then as you walk the day-to-day walk in a very hurtful, threatening, imperfect world, you have to continue to forgive.

There is just no room for unforgiveness in a close walk with Jesus Christ. Being a forgiver is the only way to truly please the God we say we love.

Chapter Seven

UNFORGIVENESS IS NOT AN OPTION

As we look at forgiveness as the key to the "Golden Chain," we see how this wonderful cycle works and how we fit into it. We must also acknowledge the absolute necessity of forgiveness.

If we want to please God, unforgiveness is not an option. Love is the foundation and forgiveness is the key, because God's greatest expression of love was offering His forgiveness through the sacrifice of Jesus.

Faith Works by Love

After we hear of His loving act of forgiveness, we must have hope that His forgiveness was real, and the faith to bring it to pass.

IFaith will keep us progressing toward our ultimate goal, and God's ultimate earthly goal for us, that of living a life of forgiveness that pleases Him and truly reflects His image.

Once we move beyond receiving His forgiveness, hoping with faith for the eternal life He's promised, we find that to live a life that pleases Him, we must keep our faith active and in operation.

Faith is a Must to Please God

I want to please God. His Word says:

"But without faith it is impossible to please him: for he that cometh to God must believe that he is, and that he is a rewarder of them that diligently seek him" (Hebrews 11:6).

Just believing in God isn't enough. To please God, I must exercise my faith—that faith that has a firm hope of His eternal reward. Even the demons believe and tremble. We need faith that recognizes who He is and is based on the unwavering hope that He will reward those who seek Him.

We mentioned earlier that the Word of God is really so simple you have to have help to misunderstand it.

ONCE I HAVE GIVEN MY LIFE TO JESUS ITS NOT NATURAL FOR ME NOT TO LOVE

The way to exercise that faith is plainly given in the Bible. It says, "faith worketh by love" (see Galatians 5:6b).

Love is the very essence of who God is.

1 John 4:8 tells us that God is love. Well, since God is love and I'm made in His image and after His likeness, then I must be love.

When we give our lives to the Lord, by faith in hope of eternal salvation through Jesus, we are able to manifest the love God intended for us to walk in when He created us in His image.

Doing What Comes Naturally

Once I have given my life to Jesus, it is not natural for me not to love. Have you ever noticed that when you get upset with someone, you're the one who gets the headache or ulcer, or puts your fist through a glass?

Why? Because you're going against your spiritual nature. As a believer, striving to please God, it's unnatural for you not to love.

Picture with me a hungry wolf prowling through the woods. He hasn't eaten for days, so he's lean and mean. He looks down through the clearing and sees Farmer Jones' sheep that has strayed away from the flock. The wolf says to himself, "That's Farmer Jones' sheep. I think I'll just herd him back to the flock."

Would it be natural for that wolf to say that? No, of course not. Tending to sheep is not in his nature – feeding off the sheep is.

Neither is it natural for you not to love if you have made Jesus your Lord.

Operating in His Love

Since faith works by love, you cannot walk in faith and please God unless you determine to operate in His love.

> **RECOGNIZING AND ACKNOWLEDGING GOD'S LOVE ISN'T ENOUGH— WE MUST ACT ON THAT LOVE**

Notice I said "operate in His love." Just acknowledging Jesus' love for you isn't enough. Just recognizing that God is a forgiver isn't enough. Even loving the Father with all your heart isn't enough. We must act on that love by loving one another through forgiveness.

Jesus Himself, in John 15, speaks repeatedly of the necessity of loving one another. Only when we are obeying this commandment of His are we truly able to walk in faith.

Love Works through Forgiveness

Faith works by love, including our love for others, and that is accomplished through forgiveness.

If we are truly walking as children of God, believers who are made in His image, we must be walking in God's love, right? We have already established the fact that the way God chooses to show us His love is through His forgiveness.

The bottom line is: Unforgiveness is not an option for a true believer.

I really want to please God, but I can only please Him by faith and this faith works by love. This love works by and through forgiveness. So, truly, FORGIVENESS IS THE KEY TO PLEASING HIM.

Chapter Eight

JESUS – OUR EXAMPLE

———∞∞∞———

God wants forgiveness for everyone in the world. It pleased Him to send His son, Jesus, that we might receive forgiveness through Him. He also wants us to please Him by being a forgiver like He is.

Jesus is both the Forgiver and our example for walking in forgiveness. While on the cross, He said,

"Father, forgive them, for they know not what they do" (Luke 23:34).

Jesus is the express image of God, the manifestation of forgiveness.

When we are determined to please God, we can always look to Jesus as our prime example. Not only was He forgiveness, He operated so powerfully in it. He, Himself, acknowledged that what He did always pleased the Father:

"Then said Jesus unto them, When ye have lifted up the Son of man, then shall ye know that I am he, and that I do nothing of myself; but as my Father hath taught me, I speak these things. And he that sent me is with me: the Father hath not left me alone; for I do always those things that please him" (John 8:28-29).

The very name we bear, "Christian," means "Christ-like." If we want to be truly committed servants of the Most High God, we need to learn what Jesus was like. We need to look at the ways He pleased the Father and then do what Jesus did. To learn what He did and what He was like, it is important to read the Word regularly. It is a living word, which is always fresh and alive in us. It is only from knowing who Jesus is and what He did that we can truly be like Him. Seeing how He pleased the Father in forgiveness will help us know how to please Him by being forgivers.

Jesus: Meek, Humble, & Powerful

Jesus was said to be meek and humble. Some have thought that meekness and humility were like weakness or weariness, being down and out. But to have meekness and humility of character means to be strong, courageous, truthful, encouraging, loving, and wise.

MEEKNESS AND HUMILITY MEANS TO BE STRONG, COURAGEOUS, ENCOURAGING, LOVING AND WISE.

I have heard meekness described as "power under control." Jesus certainly is an example of power.

In fact, He said Himself in Matthew 28:18:

> *"All power is given unto me in heaven and in earth."*

And we have already established, early in this book, that forgiveness is no ordinary power, but represents the power of God.

Jesus Walked in the Spirit

Jesus had to keep His power under control and walk in forgiveness while He was in His flesh body. If walking in a meek and humble spirit was necessary for Jesus, here on earth, to be able to operate in forgiveness, how much more do you and I have to learn to walk in a meek and humble spirit to be able to walk in forgiveness!

But there's a catch. Being meek and humble is not even in the character of the "old man" (our flesh nature). That "old man" is fearful, proud, complaining, hateful, and foolish. So before we can even begin to think about walking in meekness and humility and operating in the power of forgiveness, we must first accept the love and forgiveness God has provided for us, receive Jesus as our Savior, and become a whole new creation.

"Therefore if any man be in Christ, he is a new creature: old things are passed away; behold, all things are become new" (2 Corinthians 5:17).

Walking in His Power

If we want to walk in the same power that Jesus did, we, too, must let the old things pass away and allow all things to become new. Jesus could walk in the power of forgiveness, even while living here in human form, because He walked in the Spirit, not in the flesh.

His flesh was sorely tested, to the point that He even asked the Father if He really had to go through with His sacrifice for our sins.

"And he went a little further, and fell on his face, and prayed, saying, O my Father, if it be possible, let this cup pass from me: nevertheless not as I will, but as thou wilt" (Matthew 26:39).

Submitting to God

It wasn't that He wasn't willing to pay the price for our forgiveness, but that it was necessary for Him to face His fleshly fears and bring Himself back into the Spirit again so that He could truly surrender totally to His assignment.

When we're being tested in our willingness to be a forgiver, we, too, must submit our lives to the Father and use the power and ability that comes from His Holy Spirit living in us, so we can walk in the Spirit and not in the flesh.

Jesus, in the flesh, had to submit to God just like we do. When He was baptized, the Father was very blatant about showing His pleasure. God the Father spoke aloud as Jesus came out of the waters of baptism:

> *"And lo a voice from heaven, saying, This is my beloved Son, in whom I am well pleased" (Matthew 3:17).*

When Jesus walked on earth in the flesh, He pleased the Father. If we are to be like Him, then we need to be sure that we are doing all we can do to please the Father.

Jesus Is a Healer

When we read the scriptures, it is obvious that Jesus was a healer while He walked the earth:

> *"Bless the LORD, O my soul, and forget not all his benefits: Who forgiveth all thine iniquities; who healeth all thy diseases" (Psalm 103:2-3).*

This is true of physical healings, and we see many examples of it in the Bible, but we must remember His healing power is not limited to physical healings. His healing power also includes emotional and spiritual healings:

> *"The Spirit of the Lord is upon me, because he hath anointed me to preach the gospel to the poor; he hath sent me to heal the brokenhearted, to preach deliverance to the captives, and recovering of sight to the blind, to set at liberty them that are bruised" (Luke 4:18).*

> *"He healeth the broken in heart, and bindeth up*

their wounds" (Psalm 147:3).

And Jesus still heals today. He'll even allow us the privilege of being used as a part of His healing miracles:

"And he sent them to preach the kingdom of God, and to heal the sick" (Luke 9:2).

"And these signs shall follow them that believe; In my name shall they cast out devils; they shall speak with new tongues; They shall take up serpents; and if they drink any deadly thing, it shall not hurt them; they shall lay hands on the sick, and they shall recover" (Mark 16:17-18).

But while many are open to letting the Lord use them to pray for the sick, there is more to it than that. What we often don't realize is, when we operate in the loving forgiveness that only the Holy Spirit can lead us into, we can be used to heal wounded feelings, broken relationships, and even broken hearts, just as Jesus did.

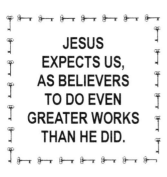

JESUS EXPECTS US, AS BELIEVERS TO DO EVEN GREATER WORKS THAN HE DID.

In fact, He expects us as believers to do even greater works than He did:

"'Verily, verily, I say unto you, He that believeth on me, the works that I do shall he do also; and greater works than these shall he do; because I go unto my Father" (John 14:12).

The example Jesus left us for being used to heal broken hearts and devastated relationships is in being a forgiver.

He could not be crucified and take His position at the right hand of God if He held any bitterness, anger, or unforgiveness toward those men who had been used to hurt, betray, and torture Him.

That is why some of His last words on earth were, *"Father, forgive them for they know not what they do."*

Jesus also made a practice of forgiving those who didn't even deserve forgiveness. When the woman who had been caught in adultery was brought before Him, she had broken the law and grieved the Lord by her actions, and had hurt others around her. Yet, instead of condemning her, He admonished her not to continue in her sin, and chose to forgive her (see John 8:11).

Forgiving as He Does

In His great love for us, He forgave us our sins when we didn't deserve it. Since we are made in His image and should be doing all we can to please Him by being like Him, it stands to reason that there will be those we will be called on to forgive who don't deserve forgiveness. And we must forgive as He does.

No matter how it is applied in our lives, in whatever circumstances, one thing seems obvious: Operating in His forgiveness is one sure way of pleasing Jesus – a living sign that we realize we are made in His image, and we appreciate His sacrifice.

Chapter Nine

OFFENSES WILL COME

There is no way that we will skip merrily through life without being hurt and offended. It is an inevitable factor of living in a world where sin has a foothold. Jesus, in Luke 17:1-5, warned the disciples to be sure that they not be the ones to do the offending, because it carries great consequences:

> *"Then said he unto the disciples, It is impossible but that offences will come: but woe unto him, through whom they come! It were better for him that a millstone were hanged about his neck, and he cast into the sea, than that he should offend one of these little ones" (v1,2).*

Then He went on to make it clear that when these offenses occur, it is the disciples' job to forgive.

> *"Take heed to yourselves: If thy brother trespass against thee, rebuke him; and if he repent, forgive him. And if he trespass against thee seven times in a day, and seven times in a day turn again to thee, saying, I repent; thou shalt forgive him" (v3,4).*

Increase Our Faith

But I take great comfort in the fact that the disciples weren't much more confident in their own ability to forgive than I am, as their response shows:

"And the apostles said unto the Lord, Increase our faith" (v5).

They made it plain that if they were to please God by walking that walk of absolute forgiveness, they needed help. It would take more faith than they had. When faced with forgiving, they needed more faith.

Some things you just come to expect, but that doesn't mean you settle for them.

So although offenses are inevitable, the Lord has what it takes for us to handle them, if we are willing to surrender ourselves to Him enough to receive that strength.

It's Normal—It's Natural

Simplistically, we might look at it this way. It's normal and it's natural for birds to fly over my head, but it's not normal or natural for birds to make a nest in my hair.

IT'S NORMAL AND IT'S NATURAL FOR GOD TO BE SENDING BLESSINGS EVERY DAY

It's normal and natural for Satan to come out every day of the year to all seven billion people on the earth with some crazy thoughts that can mess up everybody in the world. It's normal and natural, it's really no big thing.

But it's not normal or natural for me, as a child of God, to let those thoughts rest, nest, abide, and live in my head.

Expect God to Bless

It's normal and natural for God to come out every day of the year to all seven billion people on the earth with some great thoughts that can bless the socks off everybody in the world, and put socks back on them in abundance.

As a child of God, I expect it to be normal and natural for me to let those great uplifting thoughts rest, nest, abide, and live in my head.

Constantly Offended

Some folks, even though they know and love the Lord, seem to be caught in a constant, repetitive cycle of hurts and offenses.

Every time you talk with them, they have a new sad story to tell about how this person did that, or that person said this, and how much it hurt them, and how it has practically kept them from functioning,

The scripture has the answer for them, too.

In the "parable of the sower," Jesus talks about the seeds that fall on stony ground as representing those people who hear the word joyfully, but don't let it take root. Then, the minute there is a trial or attack, large or small, they are offended:

> *"But he that received the seed into stony places, the same is he that heareth the word, and anon with joy receiveth it; Yet hath he not root in himself, but dureth for a while: for when tribulation or persecution ariseth because of the word, by and by he is offended" (Matthew 13:20-21).*

Check Your Roots

When we find ourselves constantly being offended, wounded and distressed about every negative word, every perceived slight, every offhand comment, we must check our roots. We need to be rooted and grounded in God's love and in His Word (see Ephesians 3:17). Otherwise, the "soil" of our heart will not be good ground for His forgiveness to grow.

But even if we have not been the best ground, have been quick to take offense, but not quick to forgive, remember there is always help to forgive.

I know as I lay out the simple truth of God's Word about forgiveness, among those who read this will be some who will say, "But it still hurts!"

It is sad truth that many abuses, violations, betrayals, and rejections are very, very painful, even heart-breaking. I would never minimize that. But we must cling, in our times of pain and suffering, to the comfort offered by Jesus.

> *"Let not your heart be troubled: ye believe in God, believe also in me" (John 14:1).*

> *"Peace I leave with you, my peace I give unto you: not as the world giveth, give I unto you. Let not your heart be troubled, neither let it be afraid" (John 14:27).*

We cannot afford to become captive ourselves to the will of the devil by letting our pain and wounding bind us in unforgiveness.

WE CAN'T AFFORD TO BECOME CAPTIVE TO THE WILL OF THE DEVIL

Jesus says He came to heal the brokenhearted and free those who have been bruised (see Luke 4:18). He took the pain for all our hurts (see Isaiah 53:5).

A Heart of Flesh

In the Old Testament, when God made His promise to His chosen people, the Israelites, He let them know that it was He who could and would change their stony hearts, if they wanted to be His:

> *"And I will give them one heart, and I will put a new spirit within you; and I will take the stony*

heart out of their flesh, and will give them an heart of flesh" (Ezekiel 11:19).

Even believers are considered wicked until we can learn to operate in forgiveness - and the wages of sin is death (Romans 6:23). But the Lord is not pleased to have to treat us like wicked unbelievers.

For I have no pleasure in the death of him that dieth, saith the Lord GOD: wherefore turn yourselves, and live ye" (Ezekiel 18:32).

Repentance from sin, turning away from the things, thoughts, and attitudes of the world pleases God and promises us life. That's plenty of good reason to decide to let Him help us forgive.

Putting On the Armor

A sure way to be able to stand victoriously, to be able to allow God to make you into a forgiver, is to remember that the battle is the Lord's. Let's look at what we learn from Ephesians 6:12-18.

First, we see that our fight isn't with that person or persons the enemy is using to make our life miserable. It isn't against the rumors and lies that have been put out against you. It is a spiritual battle:

"For we wrestle not against flesh and blood, but against principalities, against powers, against the rulers of the darkness of this world, against spiritual wickedness in high places" (v12).

Once we realize this, we need to see the importance of being properly armed for the battle:

"Wherefore take unto you the whole armour of God, that ye may be able to withstand in the evil day, and having done all, to stand. Stand therefore, having your loins girt about with truth, and having on the breastplate of righteousness; And

your feet shod with the preparation of the gospel of peace; Above all, taking the shield of faith, wherewith ye shall be able to quench all the fiery darts of the wicked. And take the helmet of salvation, and the sword of the Spirit, which is the word of God: Praying always with all prayer and supplication in the Spirit, and watching thereunto with all perseverance and supplication for all saints" *(v13-18).*

It's All Jesus

Notice that each piece of this armor represents one aspect of who Jesus is. He is truth, righteousness, the Gospel of peace, the object of our faith, our salvation, and the Word. He is also the Great Intercessor.

When we have Jesus, we have the whole armor! That means that no matter how hard or painful the battle, we are well-equipped to win it! We just have to use what God has provided for us.

Chapter Ten

THE VICTORY BEHIND THE SCARS

"O GOD the Lord, the strength of my salvation, thou hast covered my head in the day of battle" (Psalm 140:7).

Have you ever felt like you are in a battle? Do you sometimes wonder just why it seems like the whole world is picking on you? Do you get tired of being betrayed, rejected, lied on, and emotionally battered? Don't feel like you're the only one.

The fact is, you are in a battle. It's the age-old battle of good vs. evil. Even though the enemy of our souls has been after us since conception, once we have given our hearts and lives to Jesus, we begin to feel the battle rage even more strongly. Any non-believer, or weak believer who is operating in their flesh, can be used to attack us, hurt us, wound us, or persecute us.

Notice in the scripture above that David, a man who came victoriously through many battles, recognized that it was not his own strength that kept him, but the Lord who had him covered.

A Soldier for Christ

There are many references to God's people being like soldiers, being part of an army, being prepared for battle. We have been chosen (we didn't choose Him, He chose us, remember John 15:16) to be warriors for Him, standing strong against all the tricks of the enemy. Paul prepared Timothy:

> *"Thou therefore endure hardness, as a good soldier of Jesus Christ" (2 Timothy 2:3).*

> *No man that warreth entangleth himself with the affairs of this life; that he may please him who hath chosen him to be a soldier" (2 Timothy 2:4).*

We must be willing to go through something if we are really going to serve our Lord the way He wants us to. We can't stay entangled in the arguments, bitterness, defensiveness, anger, and self-pity of this world if we truly want to please the One who called us to be warriors for Him.

It's always important to remember that even though we are in a battle, and it can get pretty brutal sometimes, we have the blessing of the Holy Spirit to draw on to heal the wounds.

WHEN EMOTIONAL PRESSURES GET TOO GREAT, IT'S GOOD TO CAST OUR CARES ON HIM

When emotional pressures get too great, it's good to remember to cast our cares on Him and let Him do the caring for us (see 1 Peter 5:7). He can handle what we're not supposed to.

Scars Can Be a Good Sign

If you have some physical or emotional scars from standing firm for Jesus, it is simply a sign that you are growing more and more like Him.

Jesus tells us to "Cheer up." He warns us that there will always be trials, tribulations, battles and unfair treatment in the world, but we have the assurance that "we win" because He has overcome the world (see John 16:33). He overcame it through forgiving, the same way we must learn to overcome our day-to-day skirmishes against the devil.

But consider the fact that the scar tissue left after a wound has been healed is usually stronger than the original skin was before the injury. Jesus, on earth, had scars, particularly on His wrists, ankles, and side. They were a sign that He had fought the battle for all of our sins, and won.

> *"But he was wounded for our transgressions, he was bruised for our iniquities: the chastisement of our peace was upon him; and with his stripes we are healed" (Isaiah 53:5).*

Expect Persecution

What some believers haven't grasped yet is that we can expect persecution. We can expect to have some people not like us, for no apparent reason. As we grow closer and closer to the Lord and become more like Him, the resentment and hatred will become even more obvious.

What we need to realize is, it's okay. It's part and parcel of belonging to Jesus. He puts it very clearly:

> *"These things I command you, that ye love one another. If the world hates you, ye know that it hated me before it hated you. If ye were of the world, the world would love his own: but because ye are not of the world, but I have chosen you out of the world, therefore the world hateth you. Remember the word that I said unto you, The servant is not greater than his lord. If they have persecuted me, they will also persecute you; if they have kept my saying, they will keep yours*

also" (John 15:17-20).

Not All Bad News

But it isn't just bad news. There are such blessings that will come because we have been willing to suffer because of our love for Jesus, that it will be well worth it. According to the Apostle Peter, we can even be glad when we take the heat for serving God, because it's part of glorifying Him by letting His glory show through you. Nothing pleases Him more.

> *"Beloved, think it not strange concerning the fiery trial which is to try you, as though some strange thing happened unto you: But rejoice, inasmuch as ye are partakers of Christ's sufferings; that, when his glory shall be revealed, ye may be glad also with exceeding joy. If ye be reproached for the name of Christ, happy are ye; for the spirit of glory and of God resteth upon you: on their part he is evil spoken of, but on your part he is glorified" (1 Peter 4:12-14).*

The Privilege of Suffering

The Apostle Paul saw it from the right perspective. He acknowledged the hardships he was going through, but also acknowledged their inability to do any lasting damage:

> *"We are troubled on every side, yet not distressed; we are perplexed, but not in despair; Persecuted, but not forsaken; cast down, but not destroyed" (2 Corinthians 4:8-9).*

This godly attitude is only possible when we are able to shut our unrenewed minds up and walk in the Spirit. It is the key to not getting caught in traps of despair and unforgiveness.

That's why it's so very important for us to learn to

become forgivers, like Jesus.

That's why God is so pleased with us when we are able to completely put away the mean and ugly things done to us and said about us by others.

Operating in forgiveness will draw us closer and closer to Him as we draw on His forgiving power. He knows it will make us strong in Him and able to withstand the things that come against us.

How pleased He is when we can stand, like Paul, and talk about the privilege of being allowed to be treated shamefully because God has entrusted us with His good news:

> *"For yourselves, brethren, know our entrance in unto you, that it was not in vain: But even after that we had suffered before, and were shamefully entreated, as ye know, at Philippi, we were bold in our God to speak unto you the gospel of God with much contention. For our exhortation was not of deceit, nor of uncleanness, nor in guile: But as we were allowed of God to be put in trust with the gospel, even so we speak; not as pleasing men, but God, which trieth our hearts"* (1 Thessalonians 2:1-4).

Enduring Afflictions

Paul spoke of pleasing God by becoming fruitful through withstanding longsuffering with joy:

> *"That ye might walk worthy of the Lord unto all pleasing, being fruitful in every good work, and increasing in the knowledge of God; Strengthened with all might, according to his glorious power, unto all patience and longsuffering with joyfulness"* (Colossians 1:10-11).

It is likely because of all he had to go through himself

that the Apostle Paul was careful to show, through his letters, the importance of keeping ourselves solid in the Lord: pleasing Him by "standing fast" (see Galatians 5:1), "enduring afflictions" (see 2 Timothy 4:5), and "fighting the good fight" (see 1 Timothy 6:12).

He realized that enduring is ultimately a positive thing, and it is necessary that we go through the battle, even though we don't like facing the battle scars, because the result of handling the offenses, the battles, with God's forgiveness and pleasing Him by standing our ground, is well worth it.

THE RESULT OF HANDLING THE OFFENSES WITH GOD'S FORGIVENESS IS WELL WORTH IT.

So instead of despairing over the battles and crying over the scars, we can look at it from the Lord's perspective. He sees you proudly bearing the marks of being His servant and is well pleased with your willingness to battle for Him and forgive your offenders.

Reviewing Key Points – Section II

11. God never asks us to do anything that _ can't accomplish.

12. What scripture tells us that without faith it is impossible to please God?_____

13. God's ultimate goal for us is to live a life of _____ which truly reflects His_____.

14. Unforgiveness is not an_____ for a true believer.

15. God wants us to please Him by being a_____ like He is.

16. Because Jesus went to the Father He expects us to do even greater works than_____ did.

17. Scars from standing firm for Jesus, are a sign that you are growing _____ _____ _____.

18. As a believer we expect_____.

19. The Lord has what it takes for us to handle offenses, if we are willing to_____ _____to Him to receive that strength.

SECTION III
COMING FULL CIRCLE

Chapter Eleven

THE HIGH PRICE OF UNFORGIVENESS

We've talked about the benefits of forgiveness, the most importance being, of course, pleasing God. But another factor it is important for us to consider is. What are the consequences of not forgiving? Forgiveness is a necessity for our walk with God, and we forgive because we want to be like Him and please Him. But what about those times we decide to wallow in our pity party and refuse to forgive or refuse to acknowledge our need to forgive, pretending everything is all right?

True, God is so forgiving that even if we choose to wallow for a bit in our pit of unforgiveness toward someone else, He is still waiting to set us back in right standing when we repent of our sin of unforgiveness. When we finally tire of paying the dreadful consequences of separating ourselves from Him, trying in vain to "pay back" an individual for their offense, and decide that pleasing Him and living in the freedom only forgiveness can offer is the only way to go, we can repent.

> *"If we confess our sins, he is faithful and just to forgive us our sins, and to cleanse us from all unrighteousness" (1 John 1:9).*

But remember the Word also warns us that the wages of sin is death (Romans 6:23). When we choose to sin, something dies. In the case of the sin of unforgiveness, it is most commonly our relationships that we destroy, because of the bitterness and anger that feed on our unforgiveness.

Growing a Bitter Root

Too many of God's people have grieved Him by letting their lack of forgiveness cause them to go from one unsuccessful relationship to another. They can't get along with their bosses, they can never develop faithful friendships, they alienate themselves from those who would want to love or encourage them.

Sometimes the bitter root grows so far that they alienate themselves from the God they love. It is a sad state of affairs in our lives if we let unforgiveness breed bitterness and anger in our spirit.

> ONCE WE CONFESS THE SIN OF UNFORGIVENESS, GOD PUTS IT AWAY LIKE ALL SIN

Once we confess the sin of unforgiveness, God puts it away like all sin. Unfortunately, the folks we have mistreated in our bitterness are not always as forgiving as they should be.

Losing what could have been quality relationships because we let the unforgiveness become a root of bitterness is a high price to pay just to wallow in our pity party for a while longer or enjoy the counterfeit pleasure of anticipated revenge.

God Takes Forgiving Seriously

We serve a God who takes forgiving seriously. It is, after all, the highest expression of love from a God who is love.

There are many references in Scripture that point out how our Lord feels about both the necessity of forgiving and the high price of unforgiveness.

When the disciples came to Jesus asking Him to teach them how to pray, Jesus told the disciples to say,

> *"Forgive us our debts, as we forgive our debtors"* *(Matthew 6:12).*

When we read the Word and realize that we can only be forgiven when we forgive, it becomes vitally important to forgive others.

> *"For if you forgive men their trespasses your heavenly Father will also forgive you: But if you forgive not men their trespasses, neither will your Father forgive your trespasses" (Matthew 6:14-15).*

Do I want to risk losing my forgiveness from God Himself over an offense done to me by some hurting person? Not on your life! The price is way too high!

We will consider several other important factors that prove that forgiveness is not worth its inflated price tag, but none is as bottom-line essential as that. We need God's forgiveness! It is our lifeline! It is our only hope of salvation!

Unforgiveness Stops Progress

To fail to forgive, or to try to put on a front of false forgiveness, is like blocking up a spring that is flowing down a mountain. It becomes useless for its intended purpose. It becomes like the Dead Sea with a stream full of life going in, but because it's not allowed to come forth it becomes stagnant and dead. That's how powerfully destructive unforgiveness can be!

When you don't forgive, you and everything around

you begins to dry up and die.

Picture a man in a car stuck in the snow or mud with the wheels spinning. He gets nowhere. That's the way we are when we try to move ahead with God but refuse to forgive. It's only when we forgive that we can get a grip and be free to move ahead in the things of God.

There are men and women of God today who wonder why they suddenly seem at a standstill. They read the Word, they pray, they praise, they go to church, but they don't feel as though they are growing – don't feel as though they are getting any closer to really knowing God like they would like to.

Do you know someone like that, or are you like that yourself? Lack of progress in things of God can most often be attributed to unforgiveness hiding somewhere in your heart. It may be some old hurt, wound, or lie the enemy has sold you from when you were a child. It may be a recent offense that you just don't seem to be able to forgive and let drop. Or it may even be that you have not forgiven yourself for some sin or hurtful action.

> **LACK OF PROGRESS IN GOD CAN OFTEN BE ATTRIBUTED TO UNFORGIVENESS HIDING IN YOUR HEART**

Being stranded on the road to nowhere, instead of moving steadily forward with the move of God, is a terrible price to pay for refusing to forgive.

You can't please God standing still. He is a God of progress, always moving from glory to glory, and it pleases Him when you are right there with Him, moving from glory to glory too!

The By-Product of Bitterness

Another by-product, or consequence, of unforgiveness is bitterness.

> *"Follow peace with all men, and holiness, without which no man shall see the Lord: Looking diligently lest any man fail of the grace of God; lest any root of bitterness springing up trouble you, and thereby many be defiled" (Hebrews 12:14-15).*

The only way we can be at peace with someone is to be walking in forgiveness, and the only way we can have that close personal relationship with the Lord that would allow us to manifest His holiness is by pleasing Him, walking as He would have us walk.

If we fail to walk in forgiveness, that root of bitterness is sure to spring up in us to trouble us.

Faith is a Must to Please God

Like a spring weed, a root of bitterness grows and multiplies when left unchecked in our spirit. It is that bitterness that causes us to have prejudices and bad attitudes toward others, and not only the person or persons who offended or hurt us.

Just like a weed in a garden can spread and choke out the healthy grass, bitterness in our soul can spread and choke out not only our willingness to forgive, but the very faith, hope, and love we so treasure.

And it doesn't just affect the person we are unforgiving toward. Notice in the verse above that it says, "thereby many be defiled." The bitterness unforgiveness carries with it will defile relationships in many areas of your life.

Choking Out Blessings

Too often, because of some old, horrific offense, our attitudes toward an entire race or gender can be soured, and many people whom the Lord has placed in our path as blessings to our life will be driven away instead by our bad attitudes.

Do you remember what I wrote earlier about the Word of God being so clear that you have to work to misunderstand it? Jesus makes no bones about the importance of forgiveness in the Word.

Consider the great teaching He gave on the difference between walking in forgiveness and unforgiveness found in Matthew 18:23-35.

Jesus Teaches on Unforgiveness

First comes the offense. The person ran up a debt it was impossible to pay:

> *"Therefore is the kingdom of Heaven likened unto a certain king, which would take account of his servants. And when he had begun to reckon, one was brought unto him which owed him ten thousand talents (Open Bible: "Fifty-two million dollars"). But forasmuch as he had not to pay, his lord commanded him to be sold, and his wife and children, and all that he had, and payment to be made" (v23-25).*

There was a stiff penalty for not paying a debt, but then the guilty party asks for mercy and forgiveness and the offended person has compassion and forgives him:

> *"The servant therefore fell down and worshipped him saying, 'Lord have patience with me and I will pay thee all.'*
>
> *"Then the lord of that servant was moved with compassion and loosed him, and forgave him the debt" (v26-27).*

But then, look at how the same person who had been given forgiveness handled an even lesser offense against himself:

"But the same servant went out and found one of his fellow servants, which owed him an hundred pence (Open Bible: "Forty-four dollars"): and he laid hands of him and took him by the throat, saying, 'Pay me that thou owest.'

"And his fellow servant fell down at his feet and besought him, saying, 'Have patience with me and I will pay thee all.'

"And he would not; but went and cast him into prison, till he should pay the debt," (v29-30).

Not only did he fail to respond to the person's plea for mercy with the same compassion he had been shown, and refused to forgive, but he decided he would take revenge and inflict punishment on the person who had offended him. Even the others around the unforgiving person were upset by his unloving act:

"So when his fellow servants saw what was done they were very sorry, and came and told unto their lord all that was done" (v 31).

The Torment of a Wicked Servant

And when the one who had poured such compassion on him and forgiven him so much heard what he had done, he was very angry:

"Then his lord, after that he had called him, said unto him, O thou wicked servant. I forgave thee all that debt because thou desirest me. Shouldest not thou also have had compassion on thy fellow servant even as I had pity on thee?'

"And his lord was wrought, and delivered him to the tormenters till he should pay all that was due him" (v 32-34).

Jesus goes on to make it very clear that this is a

direct reflection of our relationship with God when
it comes to unforgiveness;

"So likewise shall my heavenly Father do also
unto you, if ye from your hearts forgive not
everyone his brother their trespasses," (v 35).

If we do not forgive, we too will be delivered to torment-ers. Only the torment we'll endure is worse than being beaten and scourged.

It is the true anguish of living with the ugliness of unforgiveness in your heart. It is the anguish of being separated from your loving Heavenly Father by your sin of disobedience in refusing to allow Him to help you forgive.

Notice that the king called his servant "wicked" because he would not forgive. So we can see what our Lord thinks about a person who refuses to forgive. If we do not forgive, in the Lord's eyes and according to the laws of God, we are wicked servants.

The commandment to show compassion to a man who deserves good is confirmed in Proverbs 3:27:

"Withhold not good from them to whom it is due,
when it is in the power of thine hand to do it."

Love works through forgiveness. It is released first from the Father to you, then you are commanded to release it on your brother.

If we want to please God, we can't afford not to forgive. The consequence of disobeying God and reaping His displeasure is far too great a risk.

YOUR MIND
GATEWAY TO YOUR HEART

When you change

your mind

you change your

- Heart
- Life
- Possessions
- Vision
- Future
- Destiny

You BECOME

the change

Chapter Twelve

IT STARTS IN THE MIND

⸻ ∞∞∞ ⸻

"And be not conformed to this world: but be ye transformed by the renewing of your mind, that ye may prove what is that good, and acceptable, and perfect, will of God" (Romans 12:2).

The mind is the place where forgiveness is initiated, so it stands to reason that to learn how to operate in true forgiveness, we must first understand this remarkable creation.

The mind is the visionary portion of our being (hence the phrase "the mind's eye"), the basis for all physical activity.

The mind can be the place of obedience, decision, choice and rest. It is the place where decisions are made in the blink of an eye and where battles are won or lost. It is the transformer that changes fools into wise and wise into fools.

What does it mean to be transformed? It means to allow the Holy Spirit to change your carnal, worldly thinking and renew, continue to make new, your mind and heart until you have let the mind of Christ be in you (see Philippians 2).

Gateway to Your Heart

That passage of Scripture tells how we will think, act and behave when we personally renew our minds.

Your mind is the gateway to your heart. It is from your mind that all your emotions and attitudes are birthed. It is our emotional state that determines our attitudes and most of our actions.

When your unrenewed mind is in control, your emotions will swing from carnal love, lust, and greed to anger, unforgiveness, bitterness, depression, and hatred.

Walking in His Emotions

When you change your mind by allowing the Holy Spirit who lives in you to take over, you will operate in His emotions, as listed in Galatians 5:22: love, joy, peace, longsuffering (perseverance, patience), gentleness, goodness, faith, meekness, and temperance (self-control).

> **THE EMOTIONS OF THE HOLY SPIRIT LISTED IN GAL. 5:22-23 ARE THE ONLY EMOTIONS YOU NEED**

These are all the emotions you need to live a godly life, including walking in forgiveness.

Transformation Brings Proof

Read the verse in Romans 12:2 at the beginning of the chapter again. Notice that it reminds us that it is the mind that needs to be renewed, and it is that renewal, that change of mind, that causes us to be transformed.

It is after that transformation takes place that your life will be proof of the will of God, which is love and forgiveness.

When you change your heart (the heart of your mind),

it changes everything about you: your life, your possessions, your vision, your future, and even your destiny.

In fact, when you truly submit your mind to the Holy Spirit and allow Him to change your heart, you don't just see changes – you actually BECOME the change.

Depending upon whether we allow the Holy Spirit to dominate it, or we yield to our flesh, the mind is either the place of perfect peace or the seat of absolute confusion.

The "state" of our mind will determine whether we will be able to truly forgive, by obeying His leading, or stay bogged down in hurt, fear, bitterness, and unforgiveness by listening to our unrenewed mind.

"Know ye not, that to whom ye yield yourselves servants to obey, his servants ye are to whom ye obey; whether of sin unto death, or of obedience unto righteousness" (Romans 6:16).

The Tug of War for Your Mind

To a new believer, it can feel as if you are in a tug of war. Your flesh, controlled by your carnal mind, is tugging on you constantly, trying to pull you back into the sins and bondages that held you before you gave your life to Jesus.

The Holy Spirit in you is also tugging, gently and lovingly, to remind you that you are no longer a slave to sin and can stand through the temptation.

When the Apostle Paul was learning to yield his highly brilliant carnal mind to the authority of the Holy Spirit, he talked about how pulled he felt between the two (see Romans 8:18-19).

Later in his walk, however, he reached a point where he had allowed the Holy Spirit to change his mind, and died to his flesh to the point that he could say,

"I am crucified with Christ: nevertheless I live; yet not I, but Christ liveth in me: and the life which I now live in the flesh I live by the faith of the Son of God, who loved me, and gave himself for me" (Galatians 2:20).

While it feels like a tug of war, the battle that goes on between our "old" man and the "new" man is actually a full-blown war. The enemy of our soul is out to steal, kill, and destroy (see John 10:10). And we are up against not just the temptations and circumstances we see, but the spiritual forces of evil.

Apostle Paul warns us that we aren't fighting against mere flesh and blood, but against principalities, powers, the rulers of the darkness of this world, and spiritual wickedness in high places (see Ephesians 6:12).

The battle between the flesh and the spirit is absolute warfare.

The Mine Field of the Mind

In war, one of the most dangerous places on a battle-field is the mine field. These are areas where explosive devices have been hidden in seemingly neutral ground, and their purpose is to catch the enemy unaware and destroy him.

Like a natural battlefield, the spiritual battlefield of the unrenewed mind has its own mine field. Until we give our hearts to Jesus, our unrenewed mind seems to be our ally, but once we belong to Him, it becomes our enemy. The Word tells us that our carnal mind is at enmity with God:

"Because the carnal mind is enmity against God: for it is not subject to the law of God, neither indeed can be" (Romans 8:7).

As long as our unrenewed mind is in authority, those ideas, thoughts, imaginations and visions that would please God, or bring us into a closer relationship with Him, are held captive.

This is why it is virtually impossible to truly love and forgive God's way before we are born again and submit our mind to the control of the Holy Spirit.

> *"For the flesh lusteth against the Spirit, and the Spirit against the flesh: and these are contrary the one to the other: so that ye cannot do the things that ye would" (Galatians 5:17).*

It is after we have submitted our life and our mind to the Holy Spirit, that we can toss out all those negative thoughts, bitternesses, evil imaginations and selfish ambitions that feed unforgiveness. We now have the choice to make the change. With the all-powerful spiritual weapons inherent in the Holy Spirit dwelling in us, we become the conqueror in the battle being waged on the battlefield of our mind.

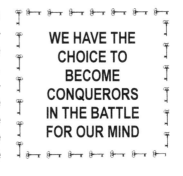

WE HAVE THE CHOICE TO BECOME CONQUERORS IN THE BATTLE FOR OUR MIND

> *"For though we walk in the flesh, we do not war after the flesh: (For the weapons of our warfare are not carnal, but mighty through God to the pulling down of strong holds;) Casting down imaginations, and every high thing that exalteth itself against the knowledge of God, and bringing into captivity every thought to the obedience of Christ" (2 Corinthians 10:3-5).*

Chapter Thirteen

RECONCILIATION THROUGH FORGIVENESS

"And all things are of God, who hath reconciled us to himself by Jesus Christ, and hath given to us the ministry of reconciliation; To wit, that God was in Christ, reconciling the world unto himself, not imputing their trespasses unto them; and hath committed unto us the word of reconciliation " (2 Corinthians 5:18-19).

The Bible tells us that God has given us a "ministry of reconciliation." The dictionary defines "reconciliation" as the act of restoring friendship or harmony, or of settling or resolving differences. Sounds a lot like the results of forgiveness, doesn't it?

It tells us that God started the reconciliation process when He reconciled us to Himself through Jesus – His first great act of forgiveness. But it also says He has given us the responsibility to continue the reconciliation process by walking in His forgiveness.

The Bible makes it clear that, ideally, the result of forgiveness will be reconciliation – the harmony and peace that comes from resolving differences and restoring relationships. That is why there are so many verses that emphasize the importance of being at peace and making peace with those who have offended you. The

Word warns us of the importance of walking in the fear of the Lord and not reacting negatively with our words when we are offended.

It tells how the Lord will hear the cries of those who not only do the right thing, but look for peace and work to make it happen:

> *"Keep thy tongue from evil, and thy lips from speaking guile. Depart from evil, and do good; seek peace, and pursue it. The eyes of the LORD are upon the righteous, and his ears are open unto their cry" (Psalm 34:13-15).*

The Bible even tells us that the Lord will not even receive our offerings unless we first make an attempt to be reconciled to those who have offended us, or whom we have offended:

> *"Therefore if thou bring thy gift to the altar, and there rememberest that thy brother hath ought against thee; Leave there thy gift before the altar, and go thy way; first be reconciled to thy brother, and then come and offer thy gift" (Matthew 5:23-24).*

Preferring One Another

It's very important to become a peacemaker and operate in His mercy (which produces forgiveness) to have more of the righteousness of the Lord activated in our lives (see James 3:17-18).

Forgiving is really putting into practice the command for us to exhibit God's love by "in honour preferring one another" (see Romans 12:10). We must be willing to humble ourselves, to give up our natural "right" to hold a grudge or seek revenge after a wrong, and instead obey our Savior's command to honor even those who have done us dirt. The act of forgiving opens the door for reconciliation of a relationship.

We must always be mindful of our attitude toward others.

When we despise anyone, it is not that person we are really despising, but God (see 1 Thessalonians 4:8).

Loving Your Enemies

Remember, it's not about you, it's all about pleasing God. He makes it painfully clear in Luke 6:27-37 how far we may need to go to truly operate in His forgiveness:

> But I say unto you which hear, Love your enemies, do good to them which hate you, Bless them that curse you, and pray for them which despitefully use you" (v27-28).

It sounds like such a tall order, and it is. If we try to do It In our natural flesh, it just won't work. The only way we can repay abuse and hatred with forgiveness and love is through the Holy Spirit living within us. We must die to our natural mind that fights so hard against God, and allow His Spirit to take authority over our soulish realm (mind, will, and emotions).

Turning the Other Cheek

And just loving them with His love is still not a clear enough act of forgiveness. Jesus goes on to say:

> "And unto him that smiteth thee on the one cheek offer also the other; and him that taketh away thy cloke forbid not to take thy coat also. Give to every man that asketh of thee; and of him that taketh away thy goods ask them not again" (v29-30).

He is actually instructing us to not fight back, and not seek restitution! That's surely nothing we can do on our own strength. Aren't you glad you don't have to count on your own strength? I know I sure am! These are definitely the times when I'm thankful that He promises to be strong in me when I am weak (see 2 Corinthians 2:9-10). Because of His strength, it is possible for the weak to say they are strong (see Joel 3:10).

He reminds us, too, that if we like to be treated fairly, if we want to have our shortcomings overlooked, if we want our sins to be forgiven, we ought to be willing to do the same for others.

Separated from Sinners

Our acts of loving forgiveness are what separate us, in God's eyes, from the sinners. It is what pleases Him because it shows that we want to be like Him:

> *"And as ye would that men should do to you, do ye also to them likewise. For if ye love them which love you, what thank have ye? for sinners also love those that love them. And if ye do good to them which do good to you, what thank have ye? for sinners also do even the same. And if ye lend to them of whom ye hope to receive, what thank have ye? for sinners also lend to sinners, to receive as much again. But love ye your enemies, and do good, and lend, hoping for nothing again; and your reward shall be great, and ye shall be the children of the Highest: for he is kind unto the unthankful and to the evil. Be ye therefore merciful, as your Father also is merciful. Judge not, and ye shall not be judged: condemn not, and ye shall not be condemned: forgive, and ye shall be forgiven:" (v31-37).*

And there are rewards for determining to please God by loving and forgiving. He will intervene and help make the situation right.

> *"When a man's ways please the LORD, he maketh even his enemies to be at peace with him" (Proverbs 16:7).*

Chapter Fourteen

FORGIVENESS WITHOUT RECONCILIATION

While forgiveness followed by reconciliation is the ideal resolution to an offense, unfortunately, your willingness to forgive does not necessarily mean there will be reconciliation. Sometimes, even when we have chosen to forgive someone, they may not care one bit about it. They may be just as ornery, hateful, and hard to get along with as they were when they were used to hurt or offend us in the first place.

> **RECONCILIATION OR NOT — WE ARE RESPONSIBLE FOR DOING OUR PART**

The Lord understood that there would be some folks, and some situations, that just aren't able to be worked out peaceably. The Apostle Paul put it this way in his letter to the Romans:

> *"If it be possible, as much as lieth in you, live peaceably with all men" (Romans 12:18).*

Notice the phrases, "If it be possible" and "as much as lieth in you." While we should always desire to bring forgiveness and peaceful reconciliation to a situation or a relationship, all we are responsible for is doing our part.

Of course, God is pleased when we are able to make peace with others, because it means we will be in a better position to be a witness for Him to a person if we are at peace with them. But, remember, when it comes down to us personally pleasing God with our walk, He's looking primarily at our hearts. If our heart is determined to be like Him and operate in His forgiveness and reconciliation, it will always please Him.

How do you respond when someone shuns your offer of forgiveness? Say a person has been lying about you to your boss, your pastor, or a new friend. You are completely blind-sided by the attack, and don't understand why they are seemingly out to hurt you. Your natural reaction is to get even, but because you want to please God and stay in right standing with Him, you make the right decision and decide to forgive the person.

AS A GESTURE OF PEACE AND FORGIVENESS, SAY SOMETHING FRIENDLY

Always Pray First

First, you will pray for them. And pray for yourself, too, in case the Lord wants to reveal something you said or did in the past that may have set you up for the offense.

You choose to forgive them, ask the Holy Spirit to help you think of them in His love, then as a gesture of peace and forgiveness you stop them when you see them and say something friendly.

Remember, you are endeavoring to be as Christ-like as possible, and when He forgives He puts the sin or offense away (as far as the east is from the west, remember?), so you don't want to even mention what the person has said about you or done to you. You may even want to preface the conversation with a peaceable, non-confrontational statement like, "I hear you may be upset with me for some reason, and I wondered what's up. Have I said or done something to offend you? If so, I'm sure sorry."

Sometimes someone is upset with you because of a "perceived" wrong, where you never actually did or said anything wrong, but they misread a word, gesture, or attitude. Even if you have searched your heart and know you did nothing to create the situation, it never hurts to humble yourself. That leaves it open for them to either apologize for saying something bad about you, rebuild a good relationship by putting it completely away and starting fresh, or rebuff your gesture of love and forgiveness.

No matter what their reaction, you have done all you could, from a heart to please God, to operate in both forgiveness and reconciliation. Can't you just see God smiling down at you?

'Move Your Toe!'

Then there are the times when the same person may offend or hurt us repeatedly.

What do we do then?

I liken it to when two people pass each other daily in a hallway. Say you're walking along, see another person coming, greet them, and keep walking. As they pass you they step on your toe. It hurts! And they just keep on walking!

You decide to let it slide, assume they just were careless, forgive them and keep moving. Good for you!

But then, the following day as you are passing in the hallway, it happens again. They tromp on your toe and just keep on trucking! It hurts something fierce, but you don't want to make a big deal out of nothing, so you forgive them once again and move along.

But if it happens repeatedly, you have an alternative to being hurt and then being forgiving.

The next time you see them coming, you need to move your toe!

Such is the case when certain relationships in our life, at work or in the family for instance, keep bringing repeated offense and hurt.

It's a good thing when you can overlook the hurt, or at least not make a federal case out of it, but just forgive and keep moving forward. But when the same person, seemingly without remorse or regret, keeps inflicting pain and distress, the best answer is to FORGIVE, YES, BUT MOVE YOUR TOE!

In other words, don't keep putting yourself into hurtful situations where you are constantly forgiving, but the situation isn't improving.

If you have forgiven in your heart, and the person to whom you offered forgiveness still wants to be in strife with you, you can relax and be at peace, knowing that the Lord is pleased with you for doing your part.

As important as it is to want to reconcile damaged relationships or resolve hurtful situations, it is even more important to know that you are pleasing your loving Heavenly Father!

How Often Need We Forgive

In Matthew 18:21, Peter came to the Lord asking,

"Lord, how oft shall my brother sin against me, and I forgive him? Till seven times?" In verse 22 Jesus says to him, *"I say not unto thee, until seven times: but until seventy times seven."*

Now that means forgiving as many as four hundred ninety times, for the same thing, in the same day.

Can you imagine that?

That's like someone stepping on your toe four hundred ninety times in the same day and you forgiving them four hundred ninety times.

And that's only the literal translation. The people in Jesus' day knew that, in their vernacular, the phrase "seventy times seven" was used to mean "more than can be counted," or "innumerable."

So He was really admonishing them to not even try to keep count, but simply keep forgiving.

No Limits

He requires us to put no limits on our forgiveness. After all, He has put no limits on His loving forgiveness of us, and He commands,

> *"...Freely you have received, freely give"* *(Matthew 10:8).*

Forgiving others is one way of expressing gratitude to the Lord for the forgiveness we have received from Him. We received it freely, and now we should be willing to give it freely.

Even when peace can't be made with the one who offended us, it helps, when we're feeling the sting of having our gesture of forgiveness thrown back in our face, to know, deep down, that God is still very pleased with us for our efforts.

Although reconciliation may be the ideal result of an act of forgiveness, the bottom line of everything in our walk is to please God. When it is in our heart to forgive, being lead by the Holy Spirit within us, that accomplishes that ultimate goal.

Chapter Fifteen

CHOOSING TO FORGIVE

Once I learned that the Word says to forgive, and recognized that it was the only way I could truly please God, I began to put forgiveness into effect in my life. It wasn't easy. It was a choice I had to make. My natural man, my flesh, doesn't want to forgive. It wants to hold on to hurts, operate in self-pity and self-righteousness, plot vengeance, or at least carry a grudge.

How can I forgive? It's a choice I make. I have hope, because I know I can get help from God. I give my grievances to the Lord and have faith that His Word is true. He said that He will carry all our burdens, all our cares. I choose to let His Spirit take authority over my unforgiving mind.

I GIVE MY GRIEVANCES TO THE LORD AND HAVE FAITH THAT HIS WORD IS TRUE

It is only through releasing the power of the Holy Spirit inside you, and walking in the Spirit of God, that you can truly forgive. Because when you walk in the Spirit you walk in His love, and His love always manifests forgiveness.

If we don't acknowledge that our flesh is dead and live by the Spirit, we will not have the hope of being able to love and forgive with God's love, and we won't walk in the faith that pleases Him. Isn't it amazing how we keep seeing that team of faith and love in every aspect of pleasing God through forgiveness?

And when we forgive, we must forgive completely. God does not forgive in part. To walk in the kind of faith that pleases God, we must reflect the image of our forgiving God. We can't afford to operate in partial forgiveness, because partial forgiveness is unforgiveness. It's like being a "little bit pregnant." You either are or you're not.

When we try to put a good face over an offense, but don't really forgive and put it away as the Lord does, we set ourselves up.

Choosing Forgiveness

It's one thing to choose to "not be mad" at the person who wounded or betrayed you. It's another to choose to forgive them for their sin against you.

It's one thing to work up a forced smile and try to be pleasant when you see someone, while just the sight of them makes your insides boil with anger and bitterness for what they've done to you or a loved one in the past. It's another to be able to stand face-to-face with some-one who has previously wronged you and look on them, or pray for them, with God's love and compassion.

When those He had done nothing but good for, those whom He'd loved and bled for, stood at the foot of that cross and mocked Jesus, He didn't say, "Just wait! You'll be sorry for what you've done to Me. I didn't deserve this treatment and I'm going to be sure My Father sends His wrath on you full force!"

He didn't look down on them and say, "It's okay. Don't worry about it. I'll be fine," and think in His heart, "Just wait until they want to come to heaven! Just wait until they need a prayer answered! They'll be sorry!"

In the natural He had that "right," didn't He? Our unrenewed mind and emotions will try to tell us that we have the right to put on a good face and hide the vengeful, bitter thoughts we're thinking until such a time as we can do something to get even.

No, Jesus said, "Father forgive them, for they know not what they do." His forgiveness was immediate, even though He was still in tortuous pain. His forgiveness was complete. The moment He spoke those words, the sins of those who mocked, scorned, beat, and crucified Him were forgiven. He gave up His natural "rights" to walk in the Spirit of God and please the Father. Can we do any less and still claim to be His?

Give the Enemy No Place

The Word of God warns us very plainly not to give the enemy any place in our lives (Ephesians 4:27). Partial forgiveness, trying to act normally when unforgiveness is eating away at us, is one of the devil's greatest openings.

> **PARTIAL FORGIVENESS IS ONE OF THE DEVIL'S GREATEST OPENINGS**

He can use it to influence our carnal mind (the one that's at enmity with God) and convince us that as long as we don't act on that anger, as long as we don't let the bitterness out, it's okay to harbor it.

"After all," he'll lie to us, "You have a right to be angry and bitter. You can fool them by pretending it doesn't matter anymore, but don't forget ever what they've done to you."

Can you even imagine what life would be like for us if God just "pretended" to forgive? If He tolerated us, trying to be loving, yet all the time seething over the pain or anger our sin caused Him?

If His love didn't manifest itself through true forgiveness, how could He bless us with salvation, let alone all the wonderful blessings He promises us in this life? Can you even imagine His wrath if He chose to keep blaming us for Jesus having to come to earth to suffer and die because we couldn't get it right? Pretty frightful thought, isn't it?

We've either given our lives to Him, or we haven't. We either love Him and want to please Him, or we don't. We either accept His sacrifice and belong to Him completely, or we don't. Our Lord and Savior is not a partial forgiver. If we want to please Him, we can't be either.

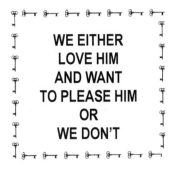

WE EITHER
LOVE HIM
AND WANT
TO PLEASE HIM
OR
WE DON'T

If you can't forgive completely, you haven't forgiven God's way at all, so you haven't pleased Him.

Maintaining a Forgiving Heart

God has made it clear to us in His Word that if we forgive, He will forgive us. But if we refuse to forgive, He will not forgive us. That is a phenomenally high price to pay. Is holding onto that grudge, that offense, that rejection, that betrayal, important enough to pay the price of losing our relationship with the Lord?

What do we do, then, when we have forgiven someone, truly forgiven them and moved on, and then six months down the road the feeling of unforgiveness comes back? Suddenly, that unforgiveness rears its ugly head and it feels just as bad, hurts just as much, as it did before. How can I forgive and really mean it and keep the feeling of unforgiveness from coming back?

It is important, at a time like that, to remember that, being made in God's image, it is unnatural not to love. Unforgiveness has strong feelings attached to it, but you must remember it is not really a part of you. It is separate from you, just like the clothing you are wearing is separate from you.

Unforgiveness Has No Right

Once I forgive, the feeling of unforgiveness may still linger, or the enemy may bring back unpleasant memories, but I must remember that it is separate from me. It has no right to me any more because I am a forgiver. I have chosen to be like my Heavenly Father, the Forgiver.

Because I have already forgiven, I must choose to use the authority God has given me in the Name of Jesus and tell the lying feeling of unforgiveness to go. The devil is in these feelings, and I need to remind that evil spirit, and myself, that these feelings no longer have any place in me.

Walking in His Spirit

If you have someone you need to forgive, it is really as simple as pleasing God by walking in His spirit of love and forgiveness. You have the hope that what the Word says is true, so you can say from your changed heart, "Father, I want to please You and be like You. Your Word says that if I forgive, You'll forgive me. So, by faith I forgive my mother, my father, my sister, my brother, my employer, the president, my wife, my husband, my child, myself or You, Father...whomever I need to forgive."

You see, it's all by faith, which is the only way either you or I can please God anyway.

I really want to please God and I can only please Him by faith. Remember, this faith works by love, and this love works by and through forgiveness.

The Highest Act of Love

We described God's forgiveness as His highest expression of love against a suffered wrong. That means that, because we are made in His image, our forgiveness toward those who have hurt us is our greatest expression of love.

Freeing someone from unforgiveness is like unlocking chains and letting someone free. It opens the door for a fresh start, just as God's forgiveness opened the door for a fresh start in our lives.

> FREEDOM FROM UNFORGIVENESS IS LIKE UNLOCKING CHAINS TO LET SOMEONE FREE

Those who are stuck with unforgiveness, and operate out of that weakness, are usually their own worst enemy. The Lord describes them as those who oppose themselves, and warns us that it is up to those of us who know Him and understand the beauty and power of forgiving, to not strive against them, but help them:

> *"And the servant of the Lord must not strive; but be gentle unto all men, apt to teach, patient, In meekness instructing those that oppose themselves; if God peradventure will give them repentance to the acknowledging of the truth; And that they may recover themselves out of the snare of the devil, who are taken captive by him at his will"* (2 Timothy 2:24-26).

They most often mistreat, abuse, reject, and abandon others because they themselves have suffered the same kind of hurt. They have allowed the bitterness and anger to seed into their spirit and turn them into mean, vindictive people, able to be "taken captive" by the enemy and used to hurt others.

Our act of love, our forgiveness as a witness of our Lord and Savior, may be the deciding factor that frees them to "recover themselves out of the snare of the devil."

Jesus made it plain:

"Greater love hath no man than this, that a man lay down his life for his friends" (John 15:13).

If Jesus was willing to literally lay down His life for you and me, shouldn't we be willing to lay down our pride, our anger, our bitterness, and our self-pity for someone else? Just think how much it will please God, especially when we know it may be crucial to their salvation.

PLEASING GOD BY COMING FULL CIRCLE

1.
FORGIVENESS –
God's highest
expression of love
against a
suffered wrong

2.
FORGIVENESS
causes LOVE
to work

3.
LOVE causes
FAITH to work

4.
LOVE works
through
FORGIVENESS

5.
By FAITH we
please God by
being forgivers

WE HAVE COME
FULL CIRCLE
& GOD IS
PLEASED

Chapter Sixteen

COMING FULL CIRCLE

The "Golden Chain" we talked about earlier in the book has come full circle when we surrender ourselves to please God by operating in forgiveness as a tangible act of loving one another.

Let's review it all very simply, in God's order.

First, God is a forgiver, and He uses forgiveness, the highest act of love against a suffered wrong, as a way to express His love to us through the sacrifice of Jesus for our sins.

Next, we grab on to the hope of His promise of eternal life, by faith, and give Him our hearts. We walk in faith because we are grateful and want to please God, and it's impossible to do so without faith.

This faith works by love. The way we express the love we have for Him is by obeying His commandment to love one another. Because we are made in the very image of God, we express our love the same way God originally expressed His love, by forgiving.

Forgiveness is the Key

And we've come full circle. Forgiveness is the key that locks the "Golden Chain" together and keeps us always moving, through every circumstance, in the center of God's will for us.

The simple illustration on the opposite page will give you a clear, simple picture of what we have been learning. Forgiveness is absolutely necessary—it is the key to pleasing God.

If you need to open your heart to allow God's Holy Spirit to move in you with His forgiveness, it is as simple as asking. The Word of God says that we have not because we ask not (see James 4:2).

Take a moment right now, wherever you are, and join me in asking the Lord to help you find and use the key of forgiveness to bring you into a position of pleasing God and experiencing the rich fullness of all He has for you:

Heavenly Father,

I come to You in the Name of Your Son Jesus Christ. I believe that He died for my sins, and as I repent, turn away from my sins, You will forgive them.

I know I'm made in Your image, Lord, and I want more of You to be reflected in my life. I want to please You. You showed Your love to me by forgiving me. I want to be able to show Your love to others by forgiving them and being free to operate in Your love and Your Holy Spirit.

I surrender my carnal emotions that would want to hang on to hurts and feel self-pity or self-righteousness. I want Your Holy Spirit to guide me into forgiving. I will choose to continue to stop the enemy of my soul when he tries to bring me back into unforgiveness. Thank You that I now have Your forgiving nature, and that unforgiveness no longer has a part in me.

I pray these things in Jesus' name, AMEN.

Reviewing Key Points – Section III

1. When you don't forgive you and everything around you begins to_____ up and_____

2. _____is a by-product of unforgiveness

3. What scripture lists the "fruit" or "emotions" of the Holy Spirit?_____

4. Your_____ is the gateway to your heart.

5. Depending on who is in control your mind is either in a place of perfect_____ or absolute _____.

6. The Bible says if we do not_____ we will not be forgiven.

7. God requires us to put no _____on our forgiveness.

8. Our Lord and Savior is not a_____ forgiver, so neither should we be.

9. Ideally (but not always) the result of forgiveness will be_____.

10. Reconciliation may be the ideal result of forgiving, but the ultimate goal is to please_____.

ABOUT THE AUTHOR

John F. Scott, Jr.

John F. Scott, Jr., has been actively ministering the Word of God and manifesting the forgiveness of God in the Denver, Colorado area for over twenty-five years.

As Chaplain of Denver County Jail, he currently serves over 2,000 inmates through counseling and Bible studies, as well as by coordinating the Volunteer Religious Staff. He has completed Mediation Training. He performs wedding ceremonies and conducts baptismal arrangements on behalf of inmates. He is also available to counsel facility staff members.

Rev. Scott was licensed in 1983 and ordained in 1984 by Divine Missionary Baptist Church in Denver, Colorado. Before accepting the assignment as Chaplain for Denver County Jail in 1998, he served as Associate Pastor of Divine Missionary Baptist Church, Mt. Gilead; and Mt. Carmel Missionary Baptist Church, and as Pastor of Rehoboth International Ministries.

Over the years he has also served others with the love of Jesus through work with local outreach ministries, including: ORCC Prison Ministry; Grace Evangelistic Ministry; Sharing & Caring Ministries; Volunteers of America; North Metro Community Services and Denver Cares Detox Center.

He has hosted and taught the Bible on the radio through a weekly program aired on KQXI Radio in Denver.

ABOUT THE EDITOR

Roxanne Ryan

Roxanne Ryan, founder of *His Voice / His Pen Ministries*, is an ordained minister who teaches, preaches, writes, and edits Christian material. She has ministered in churches and conferences in the U.S., Canada, and Nigeria, and writes and edits for numerous international Christian ministries and evangelists.

Her recent works include: "Breaking the Fall Down/Get Up Myth" (due for release in fall 2012); "Devastation to Destiny" with Sharon Wiley; "Becoming an Extraordinary Leader – Impacting Others to Lead", by Dr. Jimmie Reed; She is co-author, with Rev. Claudia Garr, of the seminar series "Journey to Triumphant Living".

Roxanne is a Life Group leader at Word of Life Christian Center in Lone Tree, Colorado, Dr. Mark T. Bagwell, pastor, and edited his book "Empowered for the Call – Understanding the Dynamics of the Anointing". She co-hosts quarterly *Spending Time with Jesus Gatherings*, teaches the Word on Revelation Speak Internet Radio, and also serves on the Board of Directors of *Redeemed Ones Jail and Prison Ministry, Inc.* as Director of Jail & Prison Ministries.

She formerly served on the ministry team at Blood Covenant Christian Faith Center in Pomona, California, and as Associate Editor of Publications and Testimony Director for *Morris Cerullo World Evangelism*, San Diego, California.

TO ORDER ADDITIONAL BOOKS
OR FOR INFORMATION ABOUT HAVING
JOHN SCOTT SPEAK TO YOUR CHURCH,
MINISTRY, OR ORGANIZATION CONTACT:

His Pen

PO Box 3093
Littleton, CO 80161
720-353-2555
hispen@msn.com

FORGIVENESS IS...

On God's Part:
The Highest Act of Love
Forgiveness is salvation
Forgiveness is covenant
Forgiveness is passover
Forgiveness is remission

On Our Part:
The Key to Pleasing God
Forgiveness is simple
Forgiveness is instantaneous
Forgiveness is a witness of obedience
Forgiveness is an act
Forgiveness is easy

Forgiveness is just three words...

"I forgive _____ "

[You fill in the blank]